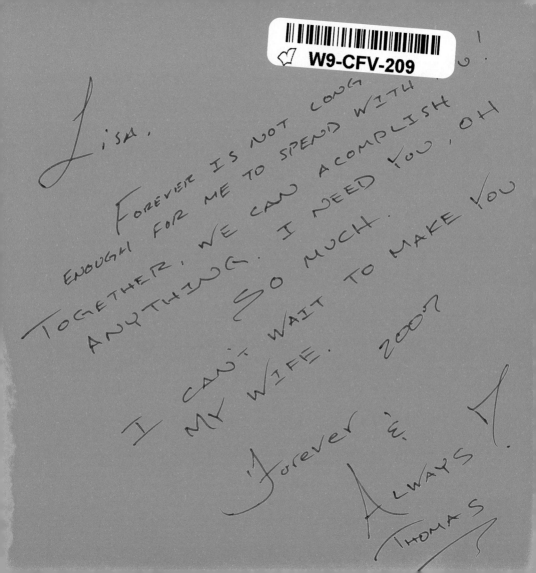

Lisa,

FOREVER IS NOT LONG ENOUGH FOR ME TO SPEND WITH YOU! TOGETHER, WE CAN ACOMPLISH ANYTHING. I NEED YOU, OH SO MUCH. I CAN'T WAIT TO MAKE YOU MY WIFE. 2005

Forever & Always

THOMAS

onward & upward

onward & upward

sayings to inspire and motivate

edited by jo ryan

Published in the United States in 2007
by Tangent Publications
an imprint of
Axis Publishing Limited
8c Accommodation Road
London NW11 8ED
www.axispublishing.co.uk

Creative Director: Siân Keogh
Editorial Director: Anne Yelland
Designer: Simon de Lotz
Production Manager: Jo Ryan

© 2007 Axis Publishing Limited

ISBN 978-1-904707-58-5

9 8 7 6 5 4 3 2 1

Printed and bound in China

about this book

Onward & Upward is an inspirational collection of phrases and sayings on the value of trying as a means of success. It is guaranteed to motivate anyone whose personal or professional life needs a boost. These words of wisdom, compiled from the thoughts of people from around the world and all walks of life, show that success comes from trying, keeping a positive attitude, relishing a challenge, and refusing to be led off track by a setback. These words will demonstrate that whatever has happened in the past, in the present and future you will succeed.

Complemented by a beautiful collection of gently amusing animal photographs, these thoughts and sayings are sure to motivate anyone to succeed, whatever their goal.

about the author

Jo Ryan is an editor and author who has been involved in publishing books and magazines across a wide variety of subjects for many years. From the many hundreds of contributions that were sent to her from people from all walks of life and all ages, from around the world, she has compiled a collection destined to foster success.

You can have a fresh start
any moment you choose.

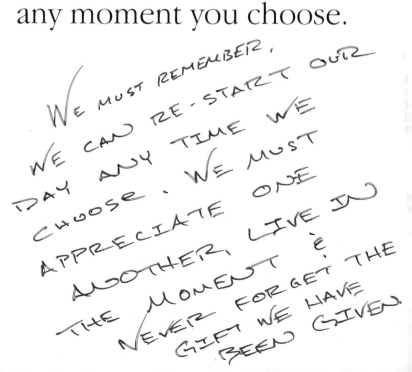

WE MUST REMEMBER,
WE CAN RE-START OUR
DAY ANY TIME WE
CHOOSE. WE MUST
APPRECIATE ONE
ANOTHER, LIVE IN
THE MOMENT &
NEVER FORGET THE
GIFT WE HAVE
BEEN GIVEN.

Be confident of
your ability…

…and tough enough
to follow through.

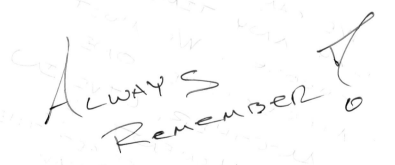

ALWAYS
REMEMBER

ooo YOU ARE LOVED.

Nobody really wins when you fight with someone you love.

To win a battle, you may need to fight it more than once.

ALSO,

WHEN TWO ELEPHANTS FIGHT ... NOTHING GETS HURT BUT THE GROUND.

SOMETIMES WHEN WE LOOSE THE FIGHT WE REALLY WIN IN THE END.

Character is doing the right thing
when nobody's looking.

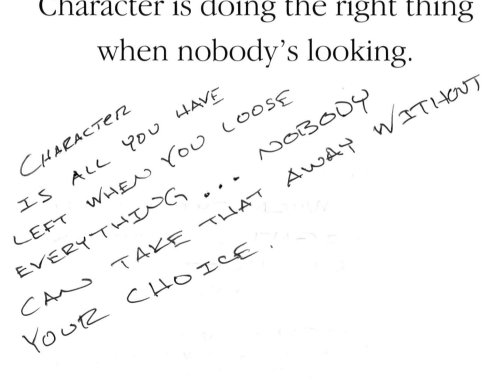

CHARACTER
IS ALL YOU HAVE
LEFT WHEN YOU LOOSE
EVERYTHING ... NOBODY
CAN TAKE THAT AWAY WITHOUT
YOUR CHOICE!

Life is an
opportunity.

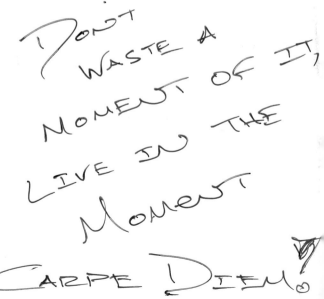

Don't waste a moment of it, Live in the moment

CARPE DIEM!

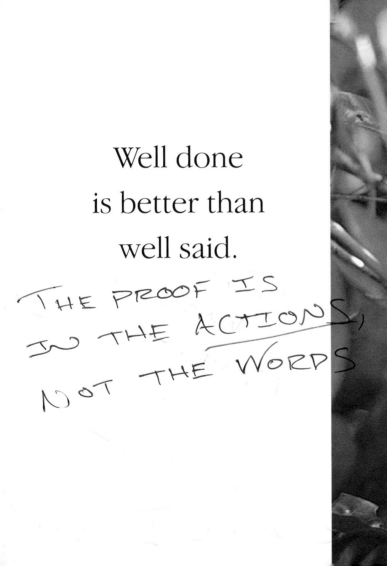

Well done
is better than
well said.

THE PROOF IS
IN THE ACTIONS,
NOT THE WORDS

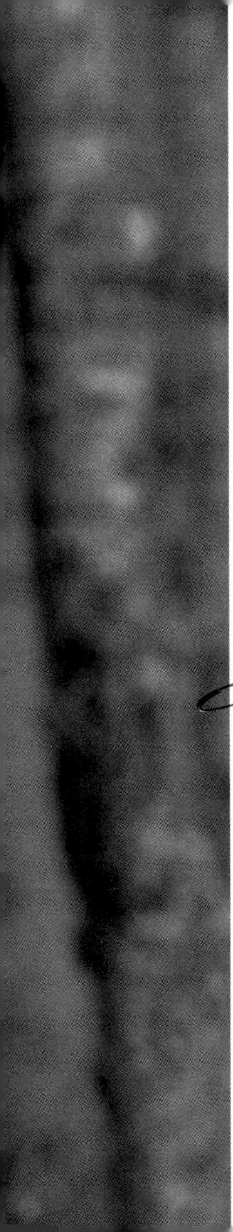

You must remain
focused on your journey
to greatness.

*Life is ABOUT THE
JOURNEY, NOT THE
DESTINATION.*

Nothing is standing
in your way...

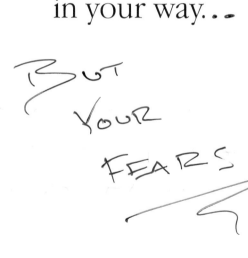

BUT
YOUR
FEARS

If you don't start
today, you won't
finish tomorrow.

THE JOURNEY
OF A MILLION MILES
STARTS WITH THE
FIRST STEP.

Fill your heart with good
things, and good things
will come your way.

So many blessings
have been
bestowed upon
us!

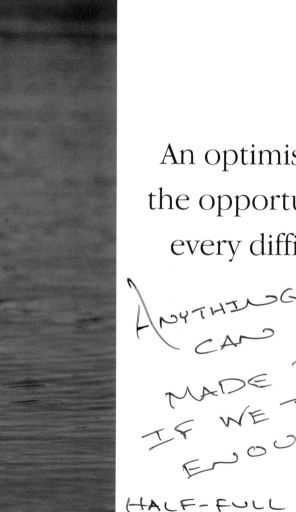

An optimist sees
the opportunity in
every difficulty.

ANYTHING
CAN BE
MADE DIFFICULT
IF WE TRY HARD
ENOUGH.

HALF-FULL BEATS
HALF EMPTY ANY!
DAY.

Scaling the mountain is
what makes the view from
the top so wonderful.

DON'T LOOSE SIGHT
OF THE FOREST BECAUSE
OF ALL THE TREES.

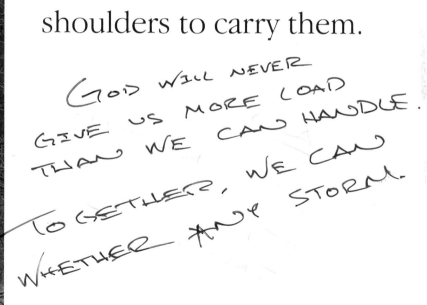

The heaviest burdens are placed on those with the shoulders to carry them.

GOD WILL NEVER GIVE US MORE LOAD THAN WE CAN HANDLE. TOGETHER, WE CAN WHETHER ANY STORM.

I can is 100 times
more important
than IQ.

WE
CAN IS
1 MILLION TIMES
MORE
IMPORTANT.

Success is a
state of mind.

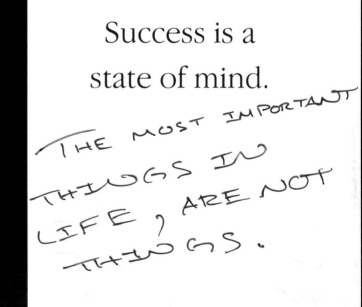

THE MOST IMPORTANT
THINGS IN
LIFE, ARE NOT
THINGS.

Many of the great
achievements of the world
were accomplished by
tired and discouraged men
who kept on working.

OPPORTUNITY IS
OFTEN DRESSED IN
OVERALLS AND
PRESPIRATION AND
NOT REALIZED BECAUSE
OF THE HARD WORK
INVOLVED.

Do not
lose courage.

We have to have courage and faith. With true faith all fears are removed and courage automatically shines through.

"Not now" fast becomes "never."

PROCRASTINATION IS SIMPLY MENTAL MASTURBATION. WE ARE SIMPLY MIND FUCKING OURSELVES.

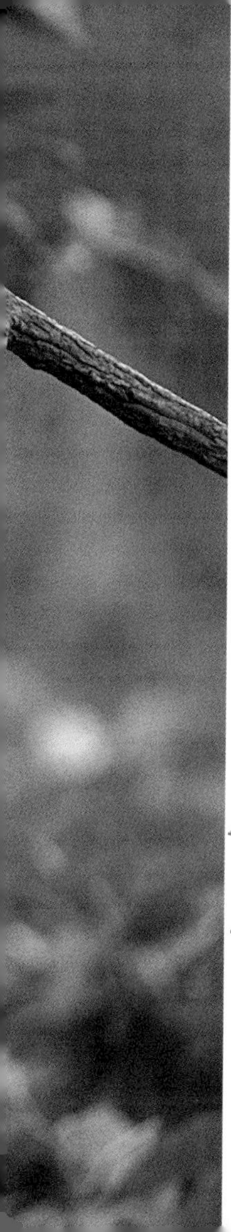

Worrying about
yesterday's failures means
today's successes will be
few and far between.

TO WORRY IS
TO BE LACKING IN
TRUE FAITH

Everyone who got
where he is had to begin
where he was.

OUR JOURNEY
TOGETHER IS LIMITLESS!
TOGETHER WE CAN
ACCOMPLISH ANYTHING.

The more you want to
get something done, the
less likely you are to
call it work.

*Love what you are doing
and it will never feel
life work.*

If you think you can,
you can.

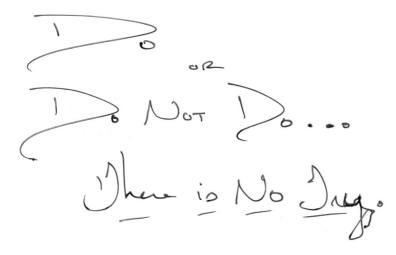

I Do

or

I Do Not Do...

There is No Try.

Things never go so well that
you should have no fear,
and never so badly that you
should have no hope.

You can have faith or
fear ... not both
with faith we are
guaranteed hope.

You can't leave
where you are until
you decide where
you want to be.

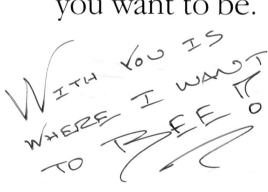

WITH YOU IS
WHERE I WANT
TO BEE !?

Making money is easy, making a difference is not.

Let's Make a Difference.

Work is the price of success.

I WANT SUCCESS. WITH US & IM WILLING TO WORK EVERY DAY FOR IT. ANYTHING WORTH HAVING IS WORTH WORKING FOR

Anyone who wastes
one hour of life does not
understand the value of life.

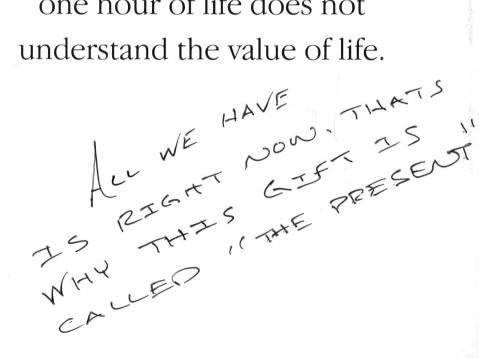

ALL WE HAVE
IS RIGHT NOW, THATS
WHY THIS GIFT IS !!
CALLED "THE PRESENT"

Much effort,
much prosperity.

Amen T.

NO EFFORT
NO PROPERITY

Don't follow
the crowd: that's
the easiest way to
get lost.

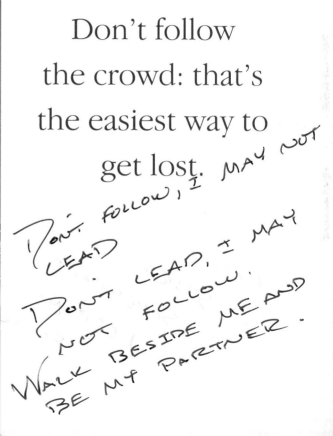

Don't follow, I may not lead.

Don't lead, I may not follow.

Walk beside me and be my partner.

You don't have to be
great to start…

…but you have to start
to be great.

GOTTA START SOMEWHERE & KEEP MOVING FORWARD.

The goal and the
price are the same: life itself.

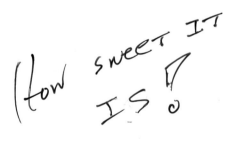

To guarantee success,
act as if it were
impossible to fail.

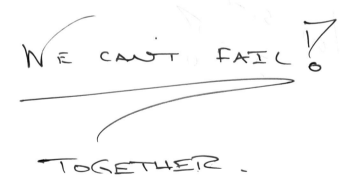

WE CAN'T FAIL!

TOGETHER.

Advance confidently in the direction of your dreams, and you'll meet with success.

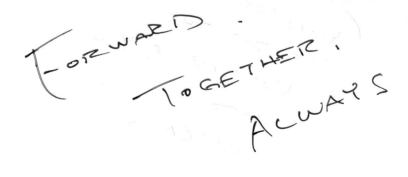

FORWARD.
TOGETHER.
ALWAYS

It takes courage to
turn out to be who
you really are.

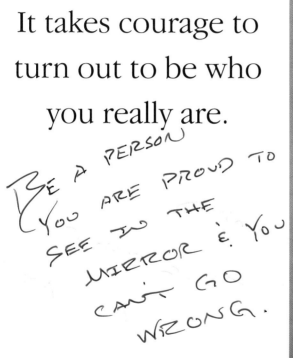

BE A PERSON
YOU ARE PROUD TO
SEE IN THE
MIRROR & YOU
CAN'T GO
WRONG.

Bad habits are like
a comfortable bed, easy
to get into but hard
to get out of.

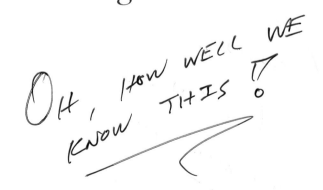

OH, HOW WELL WE
KNOW THIS !?

P.S. I LOVE SHARING A BED
WITH YOU !?

Laughing at
your weaknesses
makes you strong.

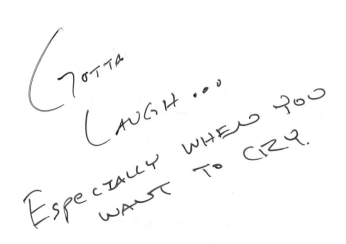

Gotta
Laugh...
Especially when you
want to cry.

The only limitation is
in your own mind.

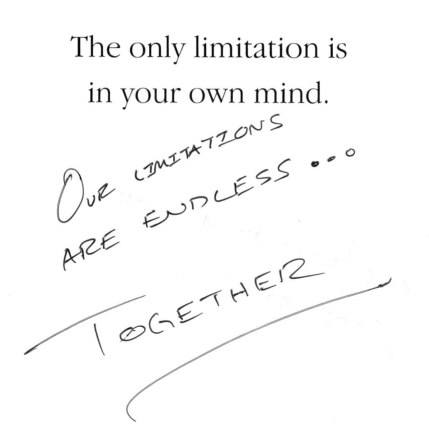

Our limitations

ARE ENDLESS ...

TOGETHER

The miracle is not to fly in the air, or to walk on the water, but to walk on the earth.

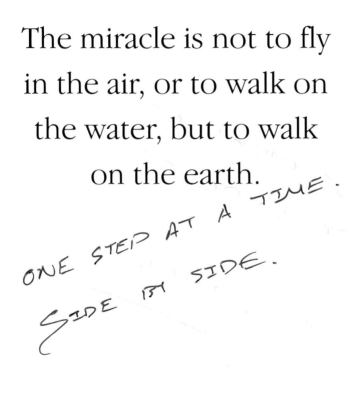

ONE STEP AT A TIME.

SIDE BY SIDE.

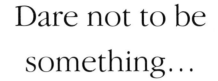

Dare not to be
something…

…dare to be someone.

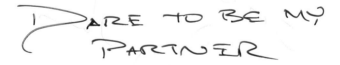

I DARE TO BE MY
PARTNER

Forever,
&
Always

Greatness is not in where we stand, but in which direction we are moving.

Forward

Joy Ethes

Believe in something
and it will happen.

TRUST IN GOD AND
BELIEVE IN US!

Obstacles are stepping
stones in disguise.

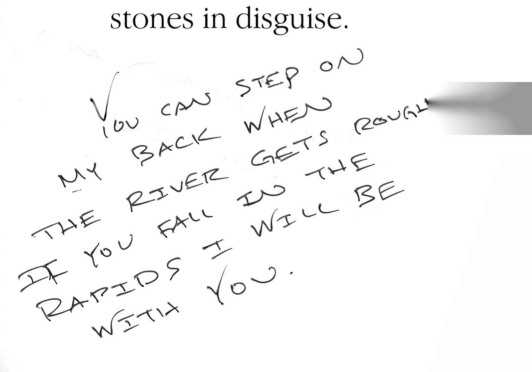

YOU CAN STEP ON
MY BACK WHEN
THE RIVER GETS ROUGH
IF YOU FALL IN THE
RAPIDS I WILL BE
WITH YOU.

What counts is not the number of hours you put in, but how much you put in the hours.

IT'S NOT THE NUMBER OF BREATHS YOU TAKE IN YOUR LIFE THAT MATTERS, IT IS THE MOMENTS THAT TAKE YOUR BREATH AWAY THAT MATTERS

Nobody got anywhere
in the world by simply
being content.

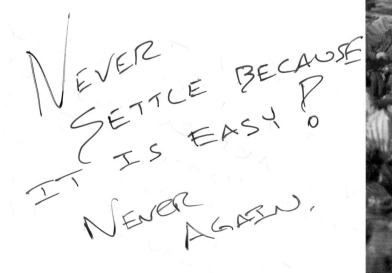

NEVER
SETTLE BECAUSE
IT IS EASY?
NEVER
AGAIN.

Enthusiasm is
faith set on fire.

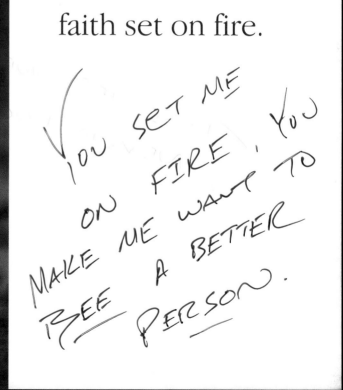

YOU SET ME
ON FIRE, YOU
MAKE ME WANT TO
BEE A BETTER
PERSON.

If you think you'll lose,
you're lost.

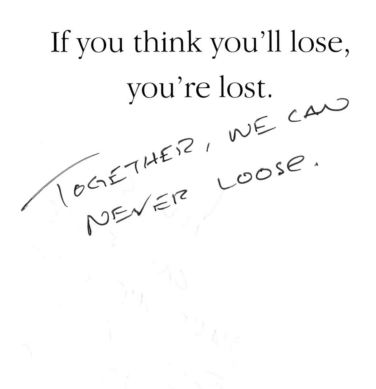

TOGETHER, WE CAN NEVER LOOSE.

Success is

failure turned inside out.

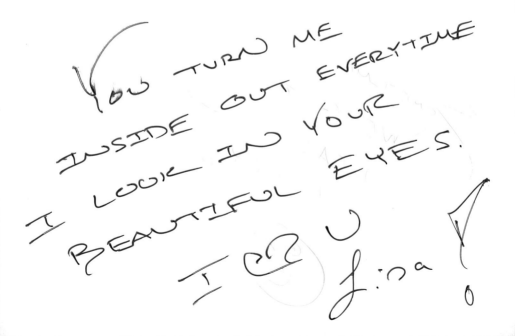

YOU TURN ME
INSIDE OUT EVERYTIME
I LOOK IN YOUR
BEAUTIFUL EYES.
I ♥ U
Lisa

The more you
sweat, the luckier
you get.

SOMETIMES
WE GET
REAL
LUCKY!

The way to succeed
is never to quit.

Never
Give Up
on Me!

Unless you are ambitious,
you do not make progress.

PROGRESS,
NOT
PERFECTION.

When the going gets tough, winners hang in until the going gets easier.

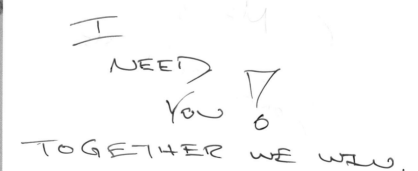

I

NEED

You ?

TOGETHER WE WILL.

Talk is cheap because
supply exceeds demand.

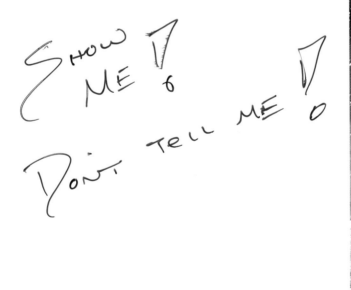

Show Me!
Don't tell me!

The best success
is built on failure.

TRY,
TRY,
AGAIN

NEVER GIVE UP.

A lost opportunity
never comes back.

NEVER
LOOSE
THIS
OPPORTUNITY,
I won't ?

The only limits
are those of vision.

WE HAVE NO
LIMITS TOGETHER .

Winners never quit
and quitters never win.

WANT TO
WIN WITH
ME?

The shortest
answer is doing.

GET ER
DONE.

Success is laughing
often and much.

Let's Be
Successful!

If you can't modify your dreams, magnify your skills.

Whatever you do, do it heartily.

WHATEVER WE
DO, LET'S DO IT
TOGETHER. FOREVER
&
ALWAYS

2007 Thomas & Dina Russell